# Small Sips of Water

## One woman's struggle through dissociation in recovery

# Small Sips of Water

## One woman's struggle through dissociation in recovery

written and illustrated by

Madeline Adler O'Conner

Launch Press, Rockville, MD

99 98 97 96 95 94 93 92 9 8 7 6 5 4 3 2 1

Library of Congress Cataloging-in-Publication Data

O'Conner, Madeline Adler, 1950-

Small sips of water : understanding dissociation in recovery /

p. cm.

ISBN 1-877872-03-2 : $6.95

1. O'Conner Madeline Adler, 1950- —Mental health. 2. Multiple personality—Patients—United States—Biography. I. Title.

RC569.5.M8026 1991

616.85'236—dc20 91-19755

CIP

# *Dedication*

First and foremost I would like to thank all the women in my life who have had the courage to feel. I have lived by their example. To live life fully and to have any chance at recovery, it is absolutely necessary that I not shut down emotionally.

To my mother, who with her passing years shines in her own courage, understanding, and acceptance. As her daughter I feel blessed that we are learning to embrace one another as sisters with a deeper wisdom in the full light of day.

To my oldest daughter who came into this world with such an open heart, I thank her for the abundance of love she gives me, and the trust she shows in me.

To my youngest daughter, who has, throughout her own journey, helped to show me the path back to myself.

# *Special Thanks*

A special thanks to my therapist Claire Jeannette who has held me over the years. She cried the tears I was unable to access. She walked with me through my darkest passageways. Without her this journey would not have been possible.

To my dear friend Ruth, who painstakingly worked with me for months, bringing my handwritten pages into legible type, who often held me when I thought I would drown in my own tears, who continues to this day to share with me my joys, confusion, and my sadness.

# Acknowledgements

My lifelong kindred spirit and dearest friend Candace, my teacher and my student, my love.

My sister Chris, for loving me through the gray plates, blue bicycle, and her toothbrush. For the big mayonnaise jar, for walking with me on the yellow brick road.

Karen Lee, for the many times she held me in my darkness, for her flower essences, for her beautiful music, for her hope.

Tanya, for standing by my side when I greeted myself for the very first time.

Peggy, who taught me that sobriety really was an option.

ila, for sharing with me her voice, her survival.

Hedi, Darah and Kelly, who affirmed for me that I was a good mother when I was filled with doubts.

Leslie for listening without judgment.

Heather, for hugging me without needing to know the reason why.

Larry and Kyle, for being such dear friends.

And every person who has remembered me.

# *Preface*

This manuscript started as a suicide note. A note to myself, really. I did not plan to share it with anyone else. I had to write down my pain, as it seemed impervious to the parts of me that wished to heal. And I needed to form concrete evidence of its unbearability, thus allowing myself to commit the act of taking my own life. Strangely, or perhaps understandably, my writing took me on a path I did not expect. I made the journey from a road of death onto a course of healing and self-awareness and self-acceptance.

I have written for over three years. I took some of the material from old journal entries. It never occurred to me that I was writing a book. I realized that I was piecing together my life, and that became very important to me.

I have put these pages into print with the dream that someone may find a shred of hope to help them with their personal struggle. If this book is able to touch just one person, then it is my belief that I have had a purpose in living through my own insanity.

There is no true ending to my story, as my healing will most probably be a lifelong process. The stronger I get in this life, the more confused I seem to be. Every question I begin to answer is replaced by several more. It seems a cruel task to get sober and stay alive in such a crazy world. However, this was my choice and continues to be so. I watch as our planet dies slowly. I refuse to be part of the living dead. I prefer to feel my pain, and the droplets of hope that sprinkle upon me when I least expect them.

# Part One

She was such a little girl, her hair thin and wispy in harmony with her frail aura, no distinct color or shape, just sort of floating, a sad dance of the fairies. Her eyes were blue; terror permeated her blinking lashes, lashes that seemed long, and thick enough to blot out the intruding world. She was so small, curled up with her bony knees covering her chest, as though protecting herself from some mammoth surge of power.

No . . . That's not true. She was a fetus, curled up, existing within a foreign uterus. She knew there was no belonging, no safety. Nights that the dogs howled, her home would be invaded by the cruel hand of the being she learned was her father. The violence invaded the womb. Her mother's pain invaded her soul. Yet she remained curled, and the invasions were buffered by the warm blood surrounding her not-yet-developed body. How she wished she could escape her early prison through a pool of blood. A gush of fluid freeing her, perhaps placed in a jar to be transported to the hospital for examination of the remaining tissue.

No . . . That's not true. She is thirty-seven years old and what? There are no words to describe her. A shell, fragile like the little girl with wispy hair, a fetus, a spirit in utero living within the embryonic fluid, within the wounded body of a woman who would forever remain a stranger. She lives each day and sleeps each night waiting for her own demise. She is running, tears streaming down her cheeks, screaming, a raging panic ripping through her body, the blades tearing at her flesh. There is no embryonic pool of blood. She is a mutilated, fragmented woman.

No . . . That's not true. She isn't running, and no screams or blood are being excreted from her body. But inside it is real. Internally, it is all coming true. She is at last dying. She can no longer withstand the pain. The memories and the phantoms too horrible to express. Her own panic slicing through her flesh. Yet to see her, she is contained. She is sitting on a bus, going to work after running away to California. She had been running all her life. From Pennsylvania, locked in the musky attic of her grandmother's house. The attic had no clear memories during those years. The memories were masked with drugs. The twinge of needles piercing through her skin was far easier to bear than the terror wrenching within her body.

Was Uncle Steven's bathroom used during the years? The bathroom where horror ran through the gushing faucets. The cold ceramic tile floor. Was the window by the toilet bowl imaginary? The toilet was real, the sink with separate faucets, one for hot water and one for cold water, that was real. The bathroom kept clean by the bronze hand of Uncle Steven's nurse. The bathtub was real. The water pouring out of the wall feeling like blades of burning ice. The tub fills slowly, to bathe the mounting *terror.*

Such a little girl. *Mommy, where are you?* She stands outside the door waiting. Tiny fingers clutching at the bouquet of freshly picked flowers. Flowers from her grandmother's garden. Pansies carefully picked just moments before. The sun still radiating from the early morning dew. She understands she must knock quietly before she enters. It smells like decay and death. A hospital bed supporting the decrepit body of an invalid. She enters . . . .

The needle feels good as it penetrates her vein. She plays a little, bringing her blood up into the syringe and pushing part way down several times, up and then down, then the final plunge. She should have made it last longer. Her body rushes. Every cell alive. She's alright now . . . for a while.

The time is late evening. The year is 1987. The month and day are unimportant. Stifled sobs coming from beneath the layers of old quilts. The bottom quilt laden with patches from her first apartment in Philadelphia. Fabric from curtains she had sewn by hand. Psychedelic prints of the sixties. She had lived alone then. Drugs glued together her daily existence. Her apartment was small, with a pullman kitchen. She had pierced her nose with a hypodermic needle. She wore a plain gold nose stud, a design she had given to a jeweler at Bailey, Banks and Biddle. Her hair was halfway down her back and frizzed. She worked at a night club near Rittenhouse Square.

Her job was her family. When the bar closed, the employees stayed till early morning. Drugs flowed as freely as the alcohol. She left only when it was safe enough to sneak through the city streets before the glare of the midday sun. There was sex then, very stoned sex. Her body, although available to others, was never available to herself. She had learned to leave her body years ago.

The bedroom was small, in the rear of the apartment, facing an alley. There was a fire escape and a music studio next door. No sun ever came into any of the rooms. But that was what she was used to. The mother had always lived in darkened rooms.

There was a bathroom in the apartment, with a tub that ran fresh, clean water. This tub would be filled with the hottest water her skin could bear. She would immerse her naked body in the steaming bath water and tie a stocking around her upper arm, holding the end between her teeth. She was always fascinated with her bulging veins. The needle was prepped as always, lying on the edge of the tub. Enveloped in steam, lending an air of mystic mountain tops, she would insert the needle, bringing up her blood. Her teeth would loosen their hold on the stocking, and she would play until the final plunge. The body rush would be magnificent, testing her heart to its maximum endurance, and she would be alright . . . for a while.

There were other patches on that bottom quilt. Her daughters' Easter bonnets and summer dresses. She always covered their heads. The bonnets were made from a homespun calico print fashioned after the provincial style of the eighteen hundreds. They also had old- fashioned straw bonnets laced with delicate silk flowers. The summer dresses she made were always of matching fabric.

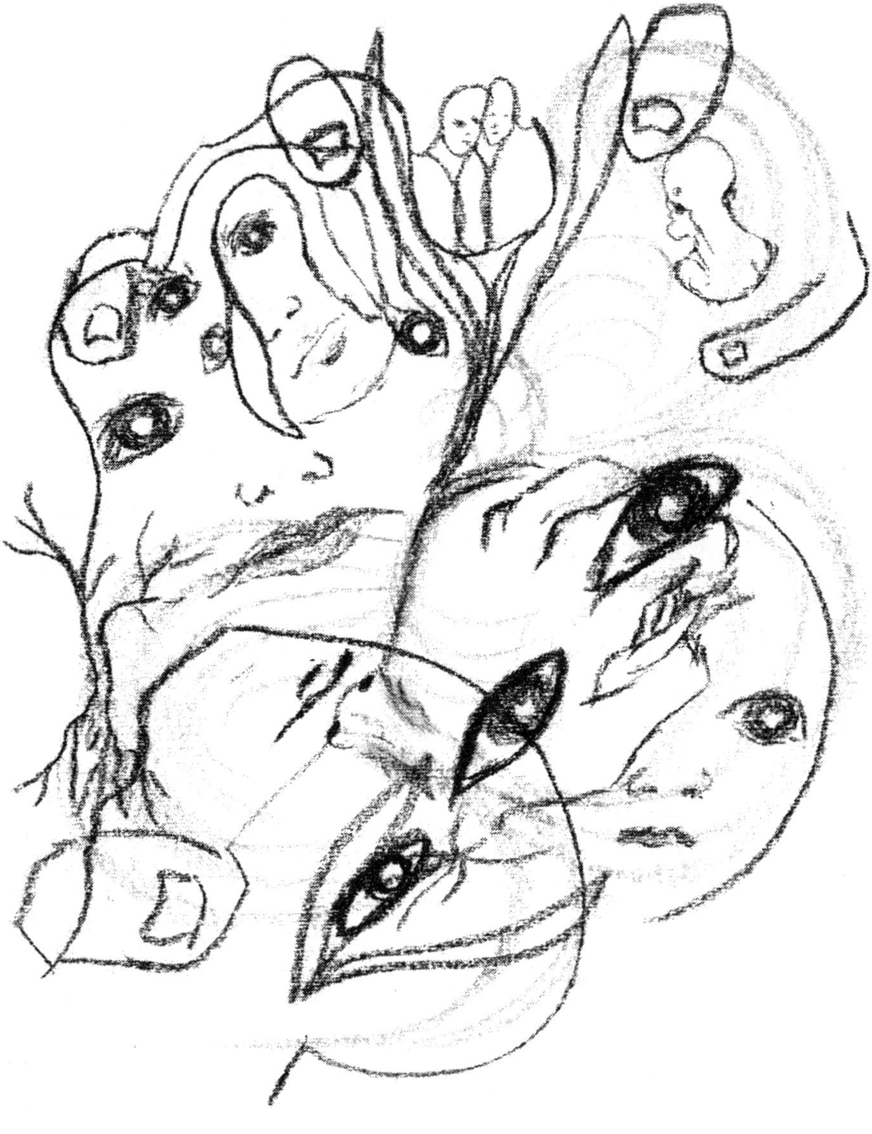

They were healthy children with fair complexions. She, the woman, wanted to be the perfect mother. She was gentle and soft, yet somehow she never really touched the little girls. It was as though she had blown a translucent bubble around each of them. She baked cookies and made soups from fresh vegetables and swallowed her valium with sips of scotch. Mommy's making wine, her children would echo as the woman stirred the ice around with her index finger. She would watch her daughters with fascination, not believing they were of her body. She wondered if this was what all mothers felt, thus making the talk of bonding and of interconnectedness simply a romantic fabrication of what motherhood was supposed to be. The daughters were dressed and cared for as though she was still playing dolls. She somehow created a whole fantasy world for them to live in. There was nothing sad allowed in their young lives. These children were even spared the normalities of cartoons—even Bambi—lest they be exposed to violence, death or any degree of sadness.

There were also patches from the two-piece bathing suit she made with a long robe to match, worn the summer she spent in Europe. And swatches from clothing worn during her time at the Calico Calf Ranch. Her torment had been increasing then; it was getting harder to numb the feelings. She was seventeen and went to the ranch to try to detox from her addictive lifestyle. Drugs weren't able to mask her pain any longer. The ranch, miles from civilization, was filled with horror for her. She'd unwittingly entered into a weird cult.

Rituals were performed—violence, anguished sex, isolation and terror, brainwashing. When she tried to leave she was berated and threatened. Her waist length hair was cropped short. She did get away from the ranch. Was she there months or a year? She couldn't remember. Much of the time was blocked from her memory. She knew it was the state police who took her away. She knew there was no violence. She remembers the rage in the eyes of the woman who was the matriarch. The mania of the house as the police walked with her out the door. It was night, darkened skies. Where was the moon? Were there visible stars? It felt silent that night, yet she knew chaos broke in the house. She was being taken away.

The second quilt was made for her daughters years before. It was flowered fabric laid out in a simple pattern. She made the quilt the same year she made the denim rag dolls with red flannel night gowns. The flannel was soft with tiny Christmas balls. She made matching night gowns for her children. The youngest daughter was blonde and her new doll had yellow yarn hair with button eyes and a smile to last as long as the embroidery thread could withstand the hugs. Her oldest daughter, then age four, had red hair. Her doll was made with long orange yarn fixed into loose pigtails. The button eyes sparkled when the light hit them. The smile was sewn cheek to cheek. She wondered whatever happened to those dolls. The night gowns had long since been outgrown. That was the last Christmas with her husband. It was the last Christmas her children would ever spend with their father. She didn't remember the man very well. She held the fear, though. He seemed so big and overbearing. The children were afraid too! The years with him passed in a fog. She drank a lot. Morning coffee laced with Scotch—always hiding her drinking. But her daughters saw, watched her pour from bottles hidden beneath the kitchen sink, behind the pots and pans and detergent. So she drank and she was alright . . . for a while.

The next quilt was the simplest. Two rose colored sheets sprinkled with an array of delicate white flowers covering an old tattered quilt rescued from the trash. She had rescued a guitar from the trash once. It was a little warped. She cleaned it up and restrung it. Her daughters were thrilled with the instrument in their lives. Mother and children would spend hours in the back room (so they wouldn't disturb the man, the children's father, the woman's husband) playing the guitar and singing songs and dressing the cat in doll clothes. In their fantasy world everyone was happy. No sadness would penetrate the lives of the children.

She herself had a guitar once, the year she went to boarding school. The memory was vague. A second hand shop in Manchester, New Hampshire. Did she ever learn to play? What ever happened to that guitar? Did it have steel strings or nylon? She didn't even know that. She was just out of the eighth grade and had a guitar. That's all she remembers, except swallowing lots of pills and smoking grass and the liquor. She wonders now if it helped, even for a while.

The quilts, like journals, remind her that she has indeed lived for years before this time. Her body curled small, riddled with pain. The sobs come from a place within her that she has long since forgotten. Like a fish pulled from the water, she thrashes and emits muffled gasps for breath. Then she settles in again to a soft crying, curled up and protected with her quilted memories. Her pink blanket has been gone for years now.

*You're being melodramatic, little Miss Sarah Bernhardt. Your head can't hurt. I never got a headache until I was married. You're going to be the death of me. I'll bet you lay awake nights dreaming up ways to put me in an insane asylum. You're the most selfish child I've ever known. Be nice. Don't hurt his feelings. You have such a vivid imagination. Stop making up stories. I'll warn you, if the doctors can't find anything wrong, I'd better never hear you complain about not feeling well again.*

Her mother's words echoed, reverberated in her head. Her skull felt like it was shrinking—a pressure making her unable to speak—pain more acute even with trying to breathe. She wanted to throw up. She lay in bed praying to the only god she knew to just let her die. Let it be a brain tumor. The aching in her stomach never seemed to go away. Her head pain grew worse and worse.

How could the hospital have found nothing wrong? They hooked her head up to some machine and they took lots of x-rays and made her drink chalky stuff. They inserted instruments into her body and stuff came from her body through tubes and into a jar while another jar was filling with more liquid. And they kept taking more x-rays. She wore a hospital gown and nothing else, and doctors kept poking at her. No one spoke much. Her mother waited all day in the waiting room, angry that she had to miss work. Again and again the words echoed. *They dammed well better find something wrong with you or else. And if they don't, young lady, I'd better never hear you complain again.* She was about eleven then and that's when the drugs started. The pain was so bad, and the doctors said it was imaginary. How could something unreal hurt so much? She supposed that if the pain wasn't real, then the pills didn't have to be real, either. There were lots of pills in those days. She never did know what they were when she took them. There were always different ones. All stolen. Stolen from the mother, the grandmother, Doctor Sherman whenever she babysat, anyone's home that she would visit. She doesn't remember now if they helped even for a while.

She still has headaches and the pains in her stomach have gotten worse. Sometimes when she's crying a lot, the pain in her stomach lessens, but it always returns in full force. She keeps her hair cropped short, close to her head except when she's not bothered to get a haircut; then it gets straggly. She wonders about when she was two, two and a half years old. What was her life like then? No memories. She'd lost all her hair, it just fell out. Stress, the doctors said. Why was a baby so stressed? It didn't make sense. Now, as an adult, she feels fat and ugly most of the time. Although she is only thirty-seven, she feels her spine and shoulders beginning to curl forward and downward, accentuating her short body.

She doesn't have sex any more. One day she decided what a waste of time her make-believe intimacy was. Her fantasies while being sexual were consumed with violence. She never understood; it just happened. She would begin to feel warm and loving toward the person she was with. Then the fear would set in—the fear and the performance. Her body would go on autopilot. As a ballerina performing an intricately choreographed dance piece, she would commit the act of sex—intercourse—what could she call it? It certainly wasn't lovemaking. It wasn't even her in the bed anymore. The only part that was hers was the internal screaming. Hands touching her arms or wrists made her feel like she was in bondage. Tenderness felt like servitude. Kisses around her neck became methods of strangulation. Her legs would go numb for no apparent reason. All the while she would be screaming on the inside. Screams her partner would never hear. And voices. The voices inside her head would whisper threats and utter humiliating words. The screaming would try to overshadow the voices to no avail. She would be split from her body. She carried only the pain. Sex when it had been with males had been most difficult. She never had sex without using. Very drunk sex. It was easier to split that way, and it was easier to block out the babble of voices living within her mind.

---

SEPT 87

Today she is out of the quilts. She sits at the kitchen table with her scotch—the bottle retrieved from its place of hiding, tucked safely away with winter sweaters. Her mind quiets. Her body numbs. A temporary place of rest. The voices occupy themselves, lending to her mind a quiet hum.

A child takes over her spirit. It is summer. There is no temperature, no time of day. Knowing it to be summer only because of lack of snow. Summer could just as easily be a weekend in this child's mind. She plays in the grass as little girls do on summer mornings. Alone. Always alone. The grass is so green next to her grandmother's garden. There is an enormous pine tree where she would hide. The fallen pine needles make for a soft bed. She spends hours under the tree. She has her very own tiny grove of lily of the valley flowers. She knows them as fairy bells. She pretends to like violets and picks great bunches for her mother, but she hates violets; she always hated violets.

Then the laughter would come. It cuts right through her. She can hear distant sounds of cartoons coming from her brother's upstairs bedroom in the grandmother's house. She doesn't remember much about her brother. The laughter roars. She curls up small under the pine tree and makes the sound go away in her head. The fairies keep her company. His laugh disappears.

She hates cartoons, except Mighty Mouse. The tune reels in her head. Mighty Mouse, Mighty

Mouse, here to save the day. As the music plays, she watches Mighty Mouse flying across the sky and swooping down to rescue the little girl mouse in a pretty dress. Mice are alright. Rats are not. She knows rats. Rats in her crib. Small body sleeping, surrounded, trapped by the wooden bars of her infant's bed. Awakening to feel a rat next to her. She has no quilts. There is nothing to protect her from the beady eyes staring directly into her, the small nose twitching, the whiskers twitching, the eyes never blinking, never breaking their stare. The panic travels through her paralyzed body. She senses the man—her father's presence in the room, but she is paralyzed now, the fear is too great and she cannot cry out.

Her scotch glass is nearly empty now as she still sits at the kitchen table. Her children are both at school, so it's safe to feel or not feel. She wonders if she should kill herself. The thoughts come to her calmly. The voices are in control. No special reason. It just seems like a good day. It's warm with a slight breeze and sunny. Seems like a good day to die. She won't tell anyone and most likely she won't die, it just seems possible. She tries to picture her children. She can't see them, their faces. She can't remember the sounds of their play. She has lost them probably, before their birth. She feels like a stranger to them.

Yet today at the moment she feels no pain. She was twice a woman large with child. How strange that was to feel life inside her womb. Foreign, unattached, and yet the unborn child had life. She felt movement in her lifeless body. She heard a story once of a pregnant woman dying in a car accident and the baby being born alive. How strange to think of dead mothers giving birth to live babies. She entertains the thought that she could have physically died, yet still birthed her daughters. And so she did. Stranger still, she remained dead yet continued to nurture them. She begins to slip into the dark tunnel—a bit more scotch just because it will feel so warm traveling into her throat and down to her stomach. Her head spins. Her gut responds with violence. She swallows.

The kitchen wasn't sunny as they sat at the small marble-topped table. She and her grandma. Was she four or perhaps five? Visiting, sharing a bottle of ale, feeling very grown-up. Sipping each morning at 11:00 a.m. before the groceries were delivered from the market.

She pours another glass of scotch. Hours pass in her life unnoticed. She carries on much of the time. Raising her daughters, talking with friends, working, going to school. Yet always there is a sense of doom. A wish for death, a pain deep inside her. And the voices are always there. Telling her she is evil, telling her to hide. She doesn't need to hide any more. She's been hiding for so many years that she doesn't know how to be real now. When sadness feels like it will consume her, she smiles and says hello to passing strangers. When the terror grabs at her every breath, she places a broader grin on her face and remarks how fine she is and isn't it a lovely day.

Looking out the window—night solitude—empty. The little girl is crying. She looks up at the stars and knows she is not alone. There is a planet way up high in another galaxy. It is a planet just like Earth. Every bush and plant are the same. The kittens born in spring are born in the same spring on that planet. The morning sun rises and the evening sun sets in the identical fashion. The music is the same, and all the strange faces that scare little girls are also way above. The other planet has oceans with waves of salt to twirl bodies in circles; it has fire engines and pine trees and even lightning bugs. All the people are duplicates of those on Earth. The little girl looks up and knows that the other one of her is there. She knows she must stay safe for her. She knows that if the other little girl way up high on that far away planet spinning in her mind, if that little girl can stay alive, then she can too!

They know about each other. No one else knows. No one would ever believe it, but she knows. It's her secret. She doesn't ever tell anyone. They would try to kill her other planet, her mirror image, the little girl exactly like her that stays alive and strong for the little girl on Earth. Tears streaming down her face, she silently looks out the window watching her planet. Waiting, waiting for Mighty Mouse to help them both.

She sits in a plush chair now, on the sixth floor of the Transamerica building in San Francisco, waiting. She is supposed to have dinner with a friend tonight, and two other women she has never met. She doesn't care much for what the evening might hold. She despises the social amenities of dinner parties and the small talk so characteristic of city bars. She copes during the evening, however, and is oddly grateful for the distraction. She is grateful, too, that the crying has stopped. Her pain is worse than usual, though. It's probably the scotch she drank—it sometimes turns on her now and makes her pain worse. Her body rejects it, disperses the vile liquid into her aging body. The alcohol still penetrates; still numbs her. For this she is thankful. But she worries about getting caught. She worries about her own alcoholism. Hours, days, weeks, months pass in her life.

Today she drank and again she got sick. She had to throw up quietly so as not to worry the children. There was blood in her vomit today. Her body is begging her to stop. Tonight she will try to give the bottle remains to a neighbor down the hall. If not, she will try to throw it away, wash it down the drain. She wonders if perhaps this is the epitome of her meager existence. She is filled with so much pain. She is sure that she is dying. She knows that she can't hide under her quilts to escape death's hand from reaching out for her. Why is it, the woman wonders, that she should always carry this sense of doom? She flips in and out of childhood memories. As a shaman, she journeys deep within her own soul, uprooting the decayed roots of the tree deceased for centuries.

It's daytime, but dark because the shade over the radiator has been drawn. It is nap time in grandma's house. There are no sounds. The sheets are cotton, crisp and white, freshly laundered and ironed. Her quilt is blue satin. But her heart is beating too fast, beating like the heart of a frightened deer in the woods, a deer found during the early morning when she hears the gun shots of hunters closing in on her. She curls up into a little ball and pulls her small body into the farthest corner of the bed. She knows she must lie very still when he enters her room. She knows she mustn't even breathe lest she feel the terror. She can feel his footsteps. Her heart beats harder and faster with the steps as they grow closer to her door. Her body is tiny now, but to her it feels huge, as though it is swollen. She feels at any moment she may begin to scream and never be able to stop screaming. Her heart beats harder and harder. She is sure he'll hear her heart beat. Maybe if she is very still and doesn't breathe he will go away. Maybe she can hide and make herself even smaller and maybe he will go away and not tickle her today.

It's nighttime and she's a woman now. The children have long been asleep. She tries to sleep but can't—pictures keep popping into her head. She is safe now, curled under her quilted journals. She is grown up and must sleep because she has to work in the morning. She tries and tries to sleep, but the pictures only get stronger.

It's so dark and quiet in the apartment tonight. The phone is off the hook and placed in the dresser drawer. She prays to her own special deity, the one she communes with from the foreign planet. She prays that she might find sleep. But the pictures keep coming back, gaining clarity. She knows not if she is awake, if she is dreaming, or if she is remembering. A large hand covers a child's mouth, and a man's arm holds the child's arm down. She sees panic in the child's face, but the pictures won't stop. Then she sees the man. Not his face. She sees his chest, his open shirt. She sees his body lowering down on top of the little girl. Then, despite the fact that she nestles inside her quilted journals, she feels the pressure of his body. She feels it on her body and understands that she is the little girl, that the terror is hers and hers alone. She feels large hands on her helpless body, her legs being forced open. She knows this man. His name is Gerald. Such a strong man, her grandmother's trusted employee. Then more pictures come, but

so fast they fade from her memory as quickly as they fade from her vision. She pulls herself out of bed and goes into the kitchen. The bright overhead light—yes, that will help, it must help. The pictures stop. Still she feels a hand between her legs. She wants to scream, but knows that would be foolish. There is no one with her. The hand is imaginary. She doesn't know how to make it go away.

Hours pass. She calms, drinking small sips of water. Her throat has closed down. She thinks of an Indian woman giving birth in silence beneath a tree, knees bent, alone birthing a new life. The pain consumed in silence. The infant crying out; the mother remaining silent. This is what she thinks of when she hears the phrase "the silent scream." She tries to no avail to go back to bed, but at every attempt to find her way to sleep, her heartbeat becomes so wild, the terror engulfing her, that she returns to the kitchen. The hand resting between her legs is gone. The kitchen is safe for a while. So she ponders what it was she saw in her mind's eye, what she felt in her body.

# Part Two

There are so many blank periods in the woman's world. Years she can not remember as though they had not existed, or she had not existed. Where had she gone? Journals were kept during those empty dark years. And photographs. But she burned much of her past. Entire books- years of her writing were burned, twice. Once in her teens, and then again in her early twenties. She collected all the written fragments of her world and put them to fire. Watching, watching—she waited, but she did not die. The pages turned to ash.

Grandma where are you? She screamed inside. She was seventeen. Strung out on meth. It was all that seemed to glue her together. She had not ventured out into the light of day for months, or was it a year of hiding, hiding in her room in the attic. She left at night into the safety of the blackened skies. Death was all she wished for. Some way to make the pain stop. Some way to find peace in her tormented mind. *Grandmother is dead now.* She knew it as she always knew death before it occurred. No reason to feed the cat or the goat, they're dead, *they're dead.* She felt like a murderess.

It was her fantasy to pour gasoline in all the rooms and torch the house, leaving, along with the memories she'd lost, a great explosion! A fire greater than the town would ever again witness. She never did commit the act she dreamt of. She burned only her journals, as though they alone held her anguish.

Now there is a new collection of writings, pages filled with who she is, shattered dreams, hopes waiting to be realized. The dates are not consistent. A week of entries, then nothing for a year, then a month or two followed again with another vast empty year. There are also drawings in the woman's life. Nightmare images exposing an ageless terror. Mutilated body parts, dark nights concealing evil, unspeakable punishments to the human spirit, the devil himself tangled in cunning lines. She had not found an answer to the grotesque images set forth on paper; only the questions.

She didn't even know the name of this artist who drew such horror. The drawing happened only during the deepest hours of the night, when there was safety from the outside world. She knew this art to be her own, yet it was not from her hand. The woman's hand drew simple flowers, tiny petals growing from delicate vines. Anyway the art stopped when she entered the "American Way of Life."

Living in the suburbs with a husband she despised and felt overwhelmed by. Time spent alone or alone with her children. Hours passing her by, sitting alone at the dining room table. A formal dining set, quite elegant, with a heavy dark pine china cabinet behind her. Treasures of her earlier days, days when she lived in her grandmother's house, inside the glass doors. The family silver—polished to perfection—tarnished in her heart. The pair of silver candlesticks unmatched due to the lack of one candle, a candle used for the children's jack-o-lantern. Her morning coffee laced with the calming scent of scotch to help ease her into the day. Where were the children? The husband slept in the next room, angrily waking with any intrusion. No sounds, no feelings, no life. The shopping had been done; bags half-empty led toward the kitchen. A blue square, two red lights and an orange hue was all that was familiar to her, and the darkness of midday. The exterior of a mild tempered home in the quiet suburbs of Philadelphia. Wall-to-wall carpeting, garbage disposal, dishwasher. The latest and best stereo equipment. It was all so very impressive.

The classic two daughters. Clean, well kept, and learning the reality of middle class bigotry. The glory of the economy car and the second family car with a white leather interior, piped-in stereo and no room for a baby seat, lest it destroy the flip-side image the husband needed to maintain.

It all ran smoothly. That was one of the rules. Life must appear to exist without fault. No waves may arise. Frank Sinatra wooed the drop-in grandparents while Al Stewart excited the teenage babysitter. How old were the children? Three and four years. *No, mommy! Don't leave! No, mommy! Don't make me stay with my daddy! No, mommy, no!* Tears, screams—terror from her four-year- old daughter-tapping into her own forgotten terror of herself as a little girl. Her child clutching desperately onto her leg as she would try to walk toward the car to go to work. Where was her child's fright from? She stopped leaving the children with the father.

Everything had to be in its proper place. There was ample room in the walk-in closet to place the vacuum cleaner and playpen. The beer mugs claimed their rightful space in the freezer, never washed with soap, always with the appropriate amount of frost covering the clear glass as she hid her scotch bottles beneath the kitchen sink and dreamt of hypodermic needles. The large screen color television projected "Sesame Street," soap operas, and appropriate evening sitcoms and dramas, ending with the nightly news. It was a dream come true. Every daughter's contentment, every mother's fancy.

It was a nightmare. An extension of her private hell. At night the husband would stagger into the house waking her from an exhausted sleep, trapping her, lumbering over her, shouting accusations and threats. She would cower into the deeper recesses of her inner soul, wanting it to end, waiting for him to go away, whether by passing out or by storming away from her in his own fury. It was the American Dream come true for every little girl born to be a woman, learning to withstand the monthly cramps, the too-clean house, the constant fatigue, the blinding headaches—learning to swallow the valium and antidepressants with her

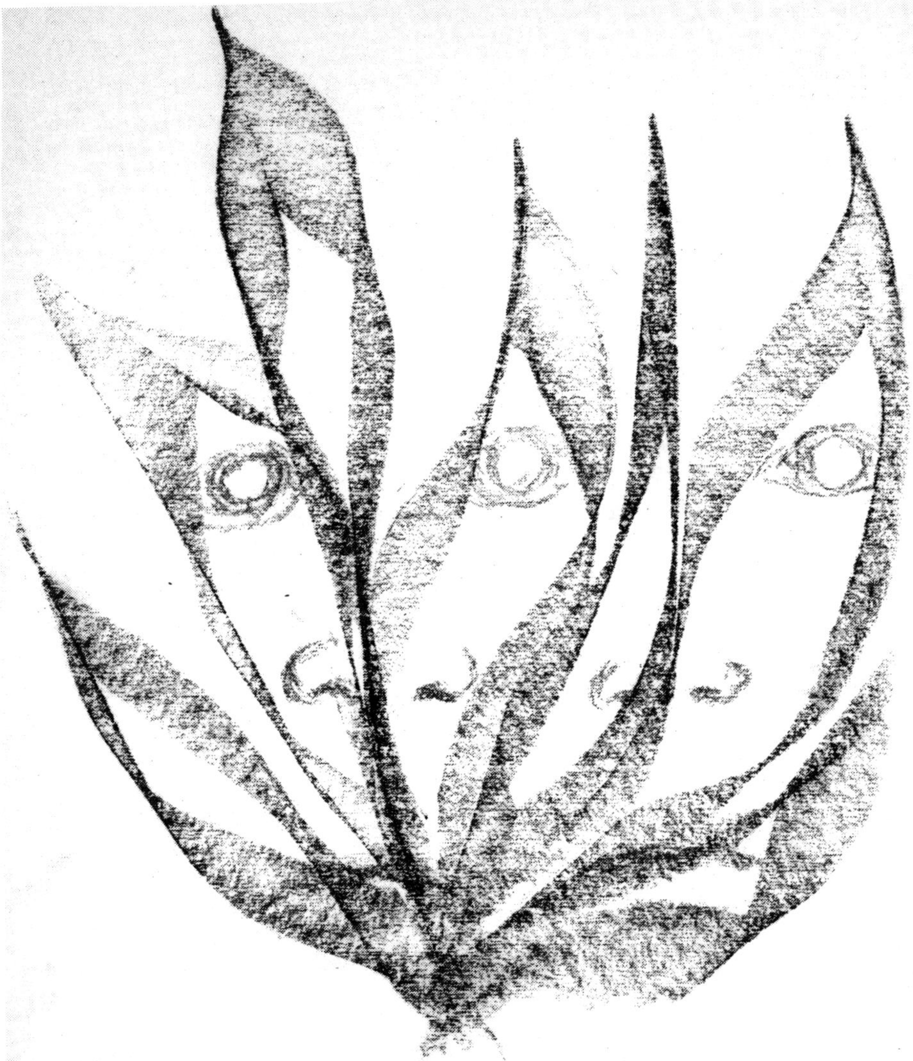

scotch, wondering if anything was real. Wondering if she could die yet.

A young child, no feelings, no awareness, reaching from her second story bedroom window, stretching her body across the open air, grasping desperately at the telephone wire. She believed in her naivete and youth that if the phone would ring, she would be electrocuted. At five years of age she was holding on for dear life or dear death. The phone never rang.

She still reaches through the nebulous mist into a distant past or perhaps a near future, transcending the phantoms dwelling in the land of unknown monsters. The pain becomes acute. A child deep inside her screams. She thrashes, kicks, bites, tears at her flesh, digs through layers of skin, blood gushing, her head bashing against brick walls, her skull mutilated. She recedes into the dark tunnel, so cold; screams echo. The walls pulsate with the throbbing of her heartbeat.

# Part Three

The journey into her scotch bottle no longer relieves her pain. Her mother's questioning voice returns to her. *Isn't there a pill for that, dear?* She can find nothing to ease the vexation, she can no longer drink herself into oblivion. Nowhere can she find solace. The voices that always babbled in her mind are gaining clarity. Daily they become more defined in their origin. They grow louder, sometimes harsh, sometimes loving. There are children murmuring questions, and at times stifled sobs can be felt. There is a cruel one inside, from whom no voice comes - no words at any rate, only a laugh. The laughter reminds her of the laughing mannequin in front of the fun house at the amusement park. Did she ever go inside the fun house? The woman can't remember. She remembers being terribly afraid of that wooden lady laughing, laughing as she clutched her aproned torso with her carved wooden hands. The laugh never sounded friendly or happy to the woman when she was a little girl. It sounded mean and ugly. The laughing lady seemed to derive pleasure from her guard post by the entrance, enticing children to walk through doors leading them into a dark, bizarre madness. She never understood how such a place could be called a fun house.

And always . . . there is the sound of a weeping child within. And a feeling of complete aloneness accompanying the little one's crying. Arguing often surfaces. Two, sometimes three voices at once, bantering with airs of frustration. The woman feels powerless over the discord within. Yet she is no longer trapped by the insanity. She feels separate and at the same time part of. She realizes that the beings dwelling in the recesses of her mind are indeed a part of her; they are her own creation, and have as much value as she herself who has housed them all these years. It is a beginning. She is aware that there are still voices she has not yet accessed. The woman is learning to recognize and differentiate between the voices that are heard. She is still unable to summon them at will. It was as though they have a will of their own and they are overpowering her.

For hours and days she sits and listens. Her mind takes her on journeys. Every voice seems to carry bizarre realities. She knows in her heart of hearts that each of these realities is truly her own. The shadows of phantoms that had once been faceless have now gained form, body, soul and living spirit. She is discovering glimpses of the treasures hidden within her despair. She is also learning the names and origins of the monsters that for decades had ravished her spirit.

She still wakes with the residue of nightly dreams, cowers in her bed wrapped in quilts, engulfed in her morning terror. She questions what it is she lives through during her sleeping hours. Are her nights filled with twisted, inconceivable fantasy or do they remind her of a long forgotten reality?

She misses her drinking—the warmth spreading from her lips down her throat, heating her belly. But mostly she misses the numbness, the loss of sensation in her body, blocking the invisible hands groping at her, hands she knows from thirty-odd years ago.

*Be nice to Gerald. Her mother's voice reverberates in her mind. Don't make up stories. Don't hurt his feelings.* She huddles in the corner of the bed in her grandmother's house, covered by her quilt of satin, waiting for the footsteps to go away, afraid to breathe, unable to voice her own screams, her spirit begging for someone to swoop down and rescue her. Her heartbeat takes on the sound of tribal drums, her throat closes, she curls smaller into her little ball of wounded flesh, forcing herself into the bedding in her childlike way to make herself invisible to his human eye. The footsteps grow closer.

She misses also the blurred vision—the images in her mind that once lacked clarity. It was easier that way. She has been sober long enough now that the numbness is beginning to wear off. Like when her grandmother would peel the skin off tomatoes. The child she once was would watch the delicate procedure. The freshly picked, vine-ripened tomatoes would be carefully washed and set aside as a pot of water was brought to a full boil. Then one by one, a tomato would be dipped through the fog of rising steam into the scalding water. This was done quickly so the fruit would not cook. Then the old woman, knife in hand, would peel the skin from each sphere. The woman watches in her mind's eye, and wonders if perhaps the tomato felt as she does now, without her protective layer of scotch or drugs. It isn't anything she can single out. It just seems like everything hurts. The body pain is tolerable, as she is most often disengaged from her own physical form. When there is pain, it seems not to exist shortly after she acknowledges the feeling.

The pain in her spirit, though, is ever present. She has hours of a manic facade of joy, where nothing seems to matter. Hours when she is untouched by even the normalities of daily living. Her body so warm as she glances into the mirror at a face with sparkling eyes. The reflection looking back, smiling in her gaiety. Not even the voices can shake her. The woman can take her anywhere in the outside world, assured that cheerfulness will confront any possible unknown adversary. But the woman always knows that at any moment the feeling can dissolve to nothingness, and the pain will return. The heaviness will flood back into her body. Disparaging voices will be convincing her of what a fool that other one is. She is an embarrassment to the rest, good thing she doesn't come often. What would people think? Who the hell does she think she is to be so unabashed in her own freedom?

The pain is wrapped in layers of sorrow and fear. The pictures in her head flash relentlessly. She no longer fights to quiet the voices or blacken the vision that is the essence of her inside world. She is learning slowly to recognize and embrace her pain. She embraces the memories as roots of an ancient tree embrace the earth. She is sustained. She walks through her darkened home searching for an ability and desire to embrace a life that has yet to happen. Still there are many demons to battle. She tries in vain to slow down the beating of her heart. If only she could listen to the voices more, help them to share the space within her mind, group them together so each could tell their stories one at a time, so each could pass out the warnings, the terror. Some are so mean to her and some laugh at her unmercifully. She needs a drink.

She begins to converse within her mind.

Voice 1: *I want a drink. Why do I want a drink?*

Voice 2: *Because you're an alcoholic.*

Voice 1: *That's not good enough. I can't accept that.*

Voice 2: *Why can't you accept it?*

Voice 1: *I don't know.*

Voice 2: *That's a cop-out.*

Voice 1: *Maybe.*

Voice 2: *We'll get back to that later.*

Voice 1: *Bitch.*

Voice 2: *So what does it feel like to you?*

Voice 1: *It feels like I'm pushing all my self-destruct buttons.*

Voice 2: *Why?*

Voice 1: *Because I want to self-destruct.*

Voice 2: *And what would that accomplish?*

Voice 1: *I don't know.*

Voice 2: *Yes, you do.*

Voice 1: *I said I don't know.*

Voice 2: *You're copping out again!*

A little one inside is crying and asking for the arguing to stop.

Voice 1: *I'm tired. I don't feel well.*

Voice 2: *The truth is you want a drink.*

Voice 1: *Yes, but I'm not drinking!*

Voice number one is getting very emotional. Her pitch is higher than before, with a slight hint of stifled sighs giving a breathless feel to her voice—and anger, the sound of anger is clearly apparent.

Voice number two, in contrast, has consistently remained calm, with a flavor of cold detachment.

Voice 2: *You have to look at why you want that drink.*

Voice 1: *I can't.*

Voice 2: *Why not?*

Voice 1: *My heart starts beating too fast and I just want to drink more.*

Voice 2: *You're running away from it.*

Voice 1: *I'm scared.*

Voice 2: *I know.*

Voice number two is sounding almost gentle for that brief moment.

Voice 1: *I want someone to hold me. I want someone to love me.*

Voice 2: *And?*

Voice number one has become quieter, almost childlike.

Voice 1: *And I don't know if I'll ever have that.*

Voice 2: *Has it occurred to you that you might not get that love until you are healthy?*

Voice 1: *Yes.*

Voice number one has a child's wonderment in it.

Voice 2: *Well.*

Voice number two has resumed her cold, matter-of-fact quality.

Voice 1: *Well, what?*

Voice 2: *Well, when are you going to do it for yourself?*

Voice 1: *I'm trying.*

Voice number one is struggling not to cry.

Voice 2: *You're not trying hard enough.*

Voice 1: *I'm lonely. I have a lump in my throat.*

Voice 2: *That means you're holding back tears.*

Voice 1: *I know.*

Voice 2: *So cry.*

Voice 1: *I can't...I just want someone to hold me...*

Voice 2: *You can't depend on someone holding you through this.*

Voice 1: *But I want someone to hold me, I get really scared. Will you hold me, please, please. I really am scared. I don't know what to do. Please?*

Voice 2: *Well, there is only one body, so I guess you're stuck.*

Voice 1: *I want somebody to hold me.*

Voice number one is sounding more and more desperate.

The little one inside rocks in the fetal position. Somewhere deep inside the woman and her voices, the little one has been listening. The little one holds herself, crying and rocking in the dark recesses of the dark room past the dark tunnel.

Voice 2: *Hang on to yourself.*

Voice 1: *I can't.*

Voice 2: *You don't have a choice.*

Voice 1: *It's not fair.*

Voice 2: *Who said life is fair?*

# Part Four

She drifts into sleeping hours. Her hours of sleep interrupted still by her nightly sweats, waking with constant trembling and a feeling of total exhaustion, accentuated by a saturated body. She sleeps on towels, and during the night wakes to dry herself off and get a fresh towel to lay upon. Sleep returns to her these nights with difficulty. Her craving for a drink, a drug, anything to ease the physical sensation, increases. Her mind wanders to the kitchen, where the cupboards go up to the ceiling. The box of hypodermic needles is gone now. Like some dream, she thrashes in wanting them back. Her therapist—she hates her therapist tonight, hates even the word. When split into two words it spells "the rapist." She'd given her therapist the needles, the odds and ends of drugs left in the house, anything she could find that she might use to get off, to escape her absurd reality. All was dropped into a grocery bag, and the bag was hand delivered to her doctor. Now it seems a dream to her, and she wants it back. Why did she stop drinking? Was it that bad? She needed to take the edge off, just a way to help her find sleep.

She remembers how clever she had been with her daughter's doctor. Suggesting that she give Nicolett the allergy shots at home—less stress for the child, she explained. Less costly, and after all, she was a single parent, and every penny counted. Made perfect sense, the doctor said, and she took home that day a new box of hypodermic needles. Her daughter did get the shots, and afterward the woman would clean the needles and return them to the highest shelf in the cupboard. She took them down occasionally, never using them on herself, just caressing them as one would a priceless antique artifact. She knows now in her heart it is just a matter of time until she can go back to drugs. The children are getting older, and then, then she will be free to numb the parts of her that the scotch can no longer reach. She is planning ahead. That's what she tells herself: it is being responsible, she is just planning ahead.

She is a very good mother. She is home when her girls get home from school. She is often sleeping. Sleeping is a nice way of saying passed out, but she is home. She is always home—Damn her! Who is she? What part of her took those needles out of the house that day?

She just wants to rid herself of some of this pain. She doesn't hate anyone, anyone except herself. She just needs to get away temporarily. Not to feel her own insidious reality. She wants the waking nightmares to stop. She thinks if she could just get high, maybe that would help for a while.

The voices return. Die, Madeline—It's time to die now. The chorus that has no name. A cluster of voices chanting from different spaces within her. They echo with their matter-of-fact statements...always the same message: *Die, Madeline...you are supposed to be dead now.* She feels caught in a whirlwind. Her fear growing as her strength dwindles, the hole looming deeper, surrounding her. The chorus of voices grows louder. She tries to question their authority, only to feel beaten by them. The darkness grows. She fears she is losing her own power. She is also losing the will to get out. The woman doesn't understand the absurd kind of insanity she is forced to wage battle with. She wonders if people struggle to stay alive in the same way. She instinctively seems to know not to betray her voices.

Her heart beat slows to the pace of a guru in a deep meditative trance as she finds a temporary rest in which to bask her fatigued spirit. For years she has harbored the fetus of her inner child, never knowing how to give her the space or the nourishment to grow. Yet the fetus survives. The woman huddles in her sleep, only with her quilts, curling into the curve of her belly.

Little children need to be taken care of, says the *nice lady.* The nice lady voice listens to the little ones when they cry. She does her best to rock them. But the *nice lady* has no body, she is only a voice. She has come out at times with other children, children living in their own bodies, bodies with arms and legs and eyes and mouths and the body parts that haven't been taken away. She has come out often to care for the woman's daughters.

She knows how to hold outside children, other people's children. She sings lullabies and reads stories and comforts them. But comforting is so complicated with the inside children, for the inside children are only voices. They have no bodies; these children can only rock in the tremors of their endless captivity within the woman's mind.

The *nice lady* always took good care of the woman's daughters. She baked cookies and enjoyed singing. She held the children's hands and played in the ocean and had tea parties. She and the children danced. She was very bright, and always seemed to know the answers the children needed to hear. She knew how to help them to feel better when they were sad. More important, she knew how to share with them their happy times. Did the children know the *nice lady* wasn't real? That she was an illusion? Or was she? What parts of the woman were true? Where did the woman end and the story people inside begin? Or was it in reverse? Could it be that the ones inside were real, and the woman was really the fallacy of the world's vision?

The woman ponders her internal questions. A gentle voice whispers inside her mind: *I am inconspicuous and undefined . . . out of focus and of misty mind. I am an illusion, an obscure manifestation, sometimes with glitter and gleam, yet I am not at all what I seem. I am any reality I wish to be, I am all the realism you cannot see.* The woman smiles to herself. Sometimes she is grateful for her voices.

The period of hunger lasts a long time for the woman. Through it she gives in to the struggle several times and buys more scotch, but it only prolongs the difficulty. Drinking just seems to take her deeper into her confusion, deeper into the hole, and she becomes sicker with the alcohol. Whether it be food or drink, her stomach tightens, refusing to let the poison or the nourishment reach the emptiness of her belly. She is becoming more disoriented, and her desperation to grasp sanity is becoming more acute. The drinking has to remain stopped. She knows that. Even the *nice lady* knew that. The children and the babies just want to sleep, to be unaware, to be anesthetized, if that's what it takes. But the children are waking up. There seems to be nothing the woman can do to quiet them. They are wandering around at times as though they are in a trance, watching each other, talking, crying and screaming.

One of the children, the *runner*, acts as a shepherd guarding her flock, rounding up the wanderers lest they stumble into the hole. The *runner* gets scared with a smell or sound from the outside world, and then runs, runs very fast, runs straight for the hole, runs into the darkness of the tunnel. Wanting only to lunge into the hole that always waits with open door. The fear the *runner* carries will go numb after a while. Then nothing, no pain, no fright, no laughter. Except from the *laughing lady*. Still, no feeling except the quiet murmur of voices calming one another down.

---

The woman is awake this afternoon. The girls (her daughters) are in the house with the usual banter of children. The woman is in the kitchen. A California day—nearly perfect—warm sun casting a glow on the chrome water faucets, dishes dripping in the drain board. The sound of MTV blending with traffic from the street below. How did the children grow so old? Wasn't it just days ago when they called her mommy and wanted bedtime songs and entertained their dolls and stuffed animals with elegant tea parties? The woman made dolls then.

The woman's daughters would come home from school and feel quite important having their very own jobs of stuffing the body parts that the woman had sewn during the day. Oh, the songs they sang together. Every song was slightly altered so as to personalize it, or changed so as to remove any hint of violence so often found in the music written by strangers. She sings in her mind, *Rockabye baby* with the new words that had been devised years ago. It was necessary to perpetuate the illusion of a fairy tale world she worked so carefully to create.

Rock a bye baby

On mama's lap

When mama rocks

The baby will clap

When baby claps,

Mama will smile,

Rocking her baby

All-ll the while.

There was no balance then. Even when Oliver, their pet guinea pig died. The children were never told about his untimely demise. Instead, the mother devised an elaborate story of how Oliver had learned so much living with the two little girls that he decided to go to school and on to college to become a teacher and move into the zoo to teach the groundhogs to read and write and become scholars. Together they would make the pilgrimage to the city zoo to visit the groundhog hill and look for Oliver.

Now the woman hears a different rhythm in her mind. The tune to "Take Me Out To The Ball Game." The words are:

Put me into the nut house

That's where I really belong

Feed me some Thorazine

And a straight jacket

I don't care

If I never get fixed.

The woman is so lost. She is waiting to die. Or is she, by some stretch of one's imagination, really waiting to live? Bodies, souls within her inner world are strewn, scattered. No light at the end of the tunnel. She wonders if all her fractions dwell within a singular tunnel or if they are held hostage in separate rooms, isolated from one another. Do they play when she cannot feel them, or do they battle the little private hells of their dreadful captivity? What about the children? The little ones inside? She feels them, but then they seem to slip away. Where are their hiding places? A sadness consumes her. All that is around her seems to be consumed with that same sadness.

She wonders what tomorrow holds. Does her near future carry the shadow of death, or does the time she has not yet wakened to, hold only more shadows?

"Mom! When's dinner?"

The woman snaps back into the moment. The sun has lost its luster. The window pulling forth warm afternoon air now allures the chill of evening. The dishes are dry, and she had not even thought of the menu for tonight. Her eldest daughter walks into the kitchen. She has a radiance about her, of a girl child undergoing the magical transformation into womanhood.

"Mom, can we have that sausage stuff you make with the mustard sauce?"

"That sounds like a good idea, but we don't have any vermouth, so it'll taste different. Do you want to help cook?"

So the woman shares time with her daughter. They talk, laugh, cry over oozing juice from chopped onions, giggle while on hands and knees picking up the full bag of egg noodles spilled onto the floor.

The woman thinks of her own mother. She was a victim all her life. Thus, when she had her own children, she was incapable of relinquishing the only role she had ever known. In order to survive, the woman's mother needed to remain victimized, childlike and dependent. Her children took on the role of parents, persecutors and rescuers. The mother knew no other way. So the woman lived her childhood as the parent to this broken woman; she fluctuated between persecuting and rescuing her own mother, yet living with the contradiction of being a victim herself, and yet motherless.

The woman looks up and smiles at her growing daughter. Somehow she and both her children are surviving. All is not lost to the woman. Her own childhood. Much of her daughter's childhood remains a blank. Where are those years hidden? Long ago she accepted the abyss of her own youth. She found it unacceptable, though, that the recall of her daughter's life voyage was also blocked. Boxes of photographs hold tidbits of those years. The girls were born a year apart, and now they are nearly teenagers. When did they cut a first tooth? Were dresses worn to the first day of school? The woman rarely attended school functions, so she never did know their teachers. They lived in many different houses in different city and country homes. The girls both seemed to know the woman, yet she often did not recognize them as her own children. How much damage occurred due to her dissociation? The girls seem to remember being little. Was it possible that the children were raised in a remotely healthy environment by the assorted fragments of her complex human being?

But they do connect, mother and daughters. They manage to breathe the same air and speak the same language. The telephone rings, and there is a blur of two young women running toward the front hall yelling, *It's for me, I'll get it!*

The woman feels the kitchen wall give way to her body as she is thrown across the room. She feels about twelve years old—her brother has walked into the greenhouse. It isn't a greenhouse as in glass walls and ceilings to promote growth of living things. It is a concrete building, newly painted green to cover the tulips the woman had painted several summers before. Large tulips with bright green stems and blood red flower tops painted clear across the white cinder block house, each flower almost two feet high. The flowers were to create a feeling of warmth, of friendliness, of safety. Were they painted on the outside because the only plant growing on the inside would be a venus fly trap? The cool dark promoted no growth. The green stems faded to a murky shade of blue over the years. Thus the house was repainted and renamed. She is on the phone, blooming in her own entrance toward womanhood. She was using language her brother doesn't approve of. Her body jerks as she feels him in her memory grabbing the phone and throwing her against the wall.

"Mom, it's for you."

Her thoughts are interrupted. There is nothing to drink.

# Part Five

The woman reflects again on her daughters. She had chosen natural childbirth so as not to inflict drugs into her daughters' systems. At least that was the reason she stated to the outside people who wondered why. The true reason was her skepticism of her own reality. At that time, she had such little faith in her own perception, that she believed that without being as present as she was capable of being, she was placing herself in danger of negating their births. She needed pictures also, because she understood how, with mere moments of time, her experiences had a way of evaporating. She didn't want the births of her daughters to become nonexistent. On every level possible to her, she wished to retain as much reality as she could.

She thinks about the labor, hypothetically now, as the feelings and clarity vanish almost simultaneously. Intellectually, she knows of the cramping, the nausea, the pressure, the physical pain of labor. Her labors were both extremely long, 14 to 18 hours, she's not sure. Both girls born posterior; with her pre-existing adhesions around her uterus, the births were that much more difficult. Yet she birthed two live children. Then she learned that the work really gets underway after the birthing. The caring and nurturing are so vital. Void of love and attention, the children would perish. Different parts of her rallied around her daughters' young lives. The woman herself missed much while the daughters were cared for by loving energy—the nursemaids, the gentle loving women living within her. The *nice lady* holds much of the memory of their infancy.

The abyss is not so dark or foreboding as she had once feared. And work it was, the journey to keep herself alive. Unwilling to follow the death chorus urging her to drive off bridges, swallow lethal doses of tranquilizers, slice into her veins with rusty blades held by shaking fingers, closing her eyes to the allure of ropes to use to hang herself. Other work in the sense of family survival. Providing food and shelter, earning a living when it felt impossible to endure one more day of struggle; settling for nothing less than keeping her daughters safe and protected. Most important, being with her daughters in the face of relinquishing custody, which seemed too uncertain for their well-being. Somehow she held onto the truth (though she knew not how) that she was the mother, and was there for them in a strong and loving manner.

Not that this work doesn't hold rewards. The rewards are great in number as they are splendid in nature. Yet as life holds many ironies, the rewards are all too often unnoticed until they have passed by. Thus it is with her life now. Just as nearly two decades ago, she has again given birth.

The labor this time was truly excruciating, and the delivery long and hard. There was no surgeon's scalpel for an episiotomy; she was forced this time by pure will and gut-wrenching work to allow the expansion to happen. Her vaginal and uterine muscles did none of the work for this birth process. It was the work of her spirit, her soul, her energy bursting forth from its suffocating cocoon, for she was giving birth to herself. No longer could she remain closed in a bud. The time had come for her to enter life.

# Part Six

She was such a little girl. Her hair thin and wispy, in harmony with her aura. Yet she is no longer the same child she had been. She is learning to be safe in her imaginary world. A world that once consumed and terrorized her with dreadful monsters. The little girl cries out loud now, no longer the subdued cries of an infant discounted. And she screams in the face of old demons. She is understanding that she is a good little girl, that little girls deserve to know gentleness in their lives. Her eyes grow wider with each new discovery. Her aura is not as pale as it once had been. She is gaining substance. The woman has given her a voice and reached out arms within to rock her. She is learning to sleep nestled in the woman's arms, tucked deeply in the recesses of the woman's mind.

That is very true, and with that truth, she is also a detective———piecing together puzzle pieces, collecting all the fragments of her life. Speaking of things she herself had once dared not hear. Things she dare not remember, she is now not only remembering, she is embracing her memories as her own truth. No longer fearful of being committed, of being called a liar, of being negated. Her realities, her truths, are no longer being felt as illicit fantasies. She is acquiring enough evidence to complete the mosaic of her past.

She is also a grown woman, quite beautiful in her own strength and endurance. She is a woman learning to be a friend to herself, learning to trust in the origins of her own pain. She is beginning to recognize her needs and desires, and to feel anger about needs that weren't met years before. She is becoming a woman who is no longer getting trapped in the fear or the anger. She is a woman courageous enough to walk the path toward healing. The foliage on that path is magnificent. Old gnarled trees bearing different fruits; some taste of sweet creamy richness, some are bitter, with a foul smell. Some are the fruits of her denial, some of the fruits of her acceptance.

This is true. Yet she is also a teenager, filled with confusion. Cautiously entering the adult world. Often uncertain of where it is she belongs. Experimenting with new ways of dressing, walking and interacting with those around her. Gleefully jumping without thought, then timidly standing back in the shadows. She is learning to focus in on herself, feeling her own energy. She is beginning to recognize dangerous situations and unsafe people. She is no longer impervious to the world surrounding her. She is learning to be a part of that world. When the outside is too hard, she retreats back to the safety of her bedroom. This room she has formed into a cocoon. Everything she and all her parts cherish have a space in that room. She burns candles, incense and smudge sticks to keep clear the flows of energy. Her music is chosen from her heart. She has an assorted array of crystals and rocks, as well as her stuffed animals. She is no longer afraid of closed doors. Her room is reminiscent of a nostalgic attic space, every corner filled with hidden treasures. Cut glass prisms hang in each window, filling the room with rainbows and sunlight. The room is warm and safe. It is her refuge as well as her birthing chamber. She is locating the many doorways to her inner world. She is growing.

The woman is also bringing from her deeper spaces the art that has always been a part of her. Her fairy world is coming to life with tiny creatures she sculpts. A land of fairies and goblins. Miniature creatures peering, opening their eyes as windows to her soul, revealing even darker spaces. Her fairies have no gender, no need to procreate, as they are creatures truly spun from magic. Haloed wreaths rest upon their head. Some have open hands embracing tiny crystal chips. Water fairies birthed in dark ocean crevasses intertwined with seaweed. Floating kelp screening out carnivorous fish and buffering underwater songs of whales that call the fairy creatures to rise to the water's surface, where the ocean glistens as polished silver in the noonday sun. The fairies hold the woman's fear of earth people. They swim in the waves of humanity's shame. Some cradle smaller fairies in their arms to protect them. The woman watches her fairy world expand, and wonders if it

1988

is an illusion of safety, or if her growing sanity is as fragile as the clay she sculpts.

As fairies come to life in her present world, so do her drawings and writings. Her dancer now is begging entrance into the outside world. So she dances. Not on a spotlight stage in New York where her childhood dreams took her. She dances alone in her room by candlelight. She dances interlocked with her own shadow. She dances as a linear form of meditation. She dances as a way of gaining continuity with her soul. She dances and feels her own fairy spirit bursting with a jubilant life force.

She reads—not as she was taught. No longer disciplining herself to read one book beginning to end. She allows herself the luxury of reading seven or eight books at a time. The floor space next to her bed has an array of novels, textbooks, writings of the old masters, and new spiritualists. Children's picture books and Chinese philosophy lying open side by side. Her assorted selves are greeting one another, learning how to co-exist, some choosing to blend with one another. All are mysteriously coming to life, whether through her art or through the blurred vision of her tears.

She still has the chorus of voices telling her it is time to die. She is resigned to their misery, understanding that their sense of futility has a right to speak also. Yet there is a stronger energy within her, one that warms the woman's spirit, one that flows richly with self-love and adoration, an energy that reminds her of the possibilities of safety and of a quieter time.

She has learned much and has spent years struggling against her own growth. She understands finally that her pain can never be as powerful as her desire for life, to grow to be all of who she is. The woman she always held inside is now able to breathe the air and feel the earth beneath her feet.

The fears have not vanished. Some of their power has been relinquished. The darkest hours of the night still hold the woman's closest friends. When there is time alone in the sanctuary of silence, she communes with her other selves, clutching hands on the front lines of her personal battles. The war has been waged, the soldiers have chosen their weapons. Swords, pistols and bayonets are replaced by truth, memory, feeling, and a comradery of the soulmates all dwelling inside the singular human form.

She still enters cautiously the unbroken ground of the outside world, believing now that dangers do exist, that she is mortal and does feel pain. The misery of the outside world saddens her and tugs at her impulse to escape from it all. There are no more drugs or drink in her life. Her mind is less muddled, her vision sharper. Her clarity is not always a pleasant sensation. Reality as a laser beam burns the retinas of her eyes, yet she heals, she feels the wound and goes on, at times temporarily blinded. Following only an echo of diminishing faith, she continues.